NBA CHAMPIONSHIPS:

↓

1999, 2003, 2005, 2007, 2014

↓

ALL-TIME LEADING SCORER:

↓

TIM DUNCAN (1997–2016):

↓

26,496 POINTS

Sprite Sprite
SOUTHWEST AIRLINES
Texas
Dodge Dealers
HEALTHSOUTH
dweiser
BUD LIGHT
WARD
21
NEW YORK
game!

THE NBA: A HISTORY OF HOOPS

SAN ANTONIO SPURS

BY JIM WHITING

CREATIVE EDUCATION CREATIVE PAPERBACKS

P.O. Box 227, Mankato, Minnesota 56002

Creative Education and Creative Paperbacks
are imprints of The Creative Company
www.thecreativecompany.us

Design by Blue Design;
production by Chelsey Luther

Printed in the United States of America

Photographs by Alamy (Sean Pavone), Corbis (Wang
Lei/Xinhua Press, Reuters, Mark Sobhani/ZUMA
Press), Getty Images (Brian Babineau/NBAE, Bill
Baptist/NBAE, Chris Covatta/NBAE, James Drake/
Sports Illustrated, Focus on Sport, Sean M. Haffey/Getty Images Sport,
Andy Hayt/NBAE, Andy Hayt/Sports Illustrated,
Wesley Hitt/Getty Images Sport, Harry How/
Getty Images Sport, Fernando Medina/NBAE,
Panoramic Images, Christian Petersen, Stacy Revere/
Getty Images Sport, Joe Robbins/Getty Images
Sport, Rogers Photo Archive, Bob Rosato/Sports
Illustrated, Gregory Shamus/Getty Images Sport,
Kent Smith/NBAE, University of California Los
Angeles/Collegiate Images, Rocky Widner/NBAE)

Library of Congress Cataloging-in-Publication Data

Names: Whiting, Jim, 1943- author.

Title: San Antonio Spurs / Jim Whiting.

Series: The NBA: A History of Hoops.

Includes bibliographical references and index.

Summary: This high-interest title summarizes the
history of the San Antonio Spurs professional
basketball team, highlighting memorable events
and noteworthy players such as Tim Duncan.

Identifiers: LCCN 2017010247 / ISBN 978-1-60818-
861-1 (hardcover) / ISBN 978-1-62832-464-8
(pbk) / ISBN 978-1-56660-909-8 (eBook)

Subjects: LCSH: 1. San Antonio Spurs
(Basketball team)—History—Juvenile
literature. 2. San Antonio Spurs (Basketball
team)—Biography—Juvenile literature.

Classification: LCC GV885.52.S26 W55 2017 /
DDC 796.323/6409764351—dc23

CCSS: RI.4.1, 2, 3, 4; RI.5.1, 2, 4; RI.6.1, 2, 3;
RF.4.3, 4; RF.5.3, 4; RH. 6-8. 4, 5, 7

First Edition HC 9 8 7 6 5 4 3 2 1

First Edition PBK 9 8 7 6 5 4 3 2 1

CONTENTS

LEGENDS OF THE HARDWOOD

One of the nation's oldest cities, **SAN ANTONIO** is famous for its River Walk and the historic Fort Alamo.

9

THE ICE AGE
IN TEXAS

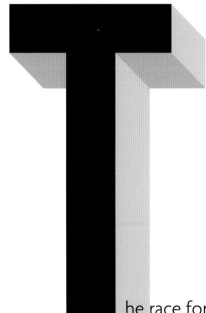

The race for the 1977–78 National Basketball Association (NBA) scoring title came down to the season's final day. San Antonio Spurs guard George Gervin held a slight lead. David Thompson of

Guard **GEORGE GERVIN** was known as "Iceman" because he kept his cool at crucial moments.

the Denver Nuggets was close behind. Thompson broke loose for 73 points in an afternoon game. It is the fourth-highest single-game performance in NBA history. It vaulted him into the lead. Gervin needed to score 58 points that evening against the New Orleans Jazz. Gervin missed his first six shots. Then "The Iceman," as many people called him, heated up. He scored 20 points in the rest of the first quarter. He added 33 in the second quarter. "I was just in a zone," he said. "I was like Casper the Friendly Ghost. I was going through guys." He scored the five remaining points he needed midway through the third quarter. "Let me go on and get a couple more points, just in case they miscalculated," Gervin told the coaches. He added 5 more for a total of 63. Then he took the rest of the night off. He finished the season with an average of 27.22 points a game. Thompson had 27.15. It remains the closest finish in NBA history.

Gervin was the Spurs' first big star. The franchise began about a decade earlier and several hundred miles away in Dallas. In 1967, the American Basketball Association (ABA) got underway as a rival to the NBA. One team was the Dallas Chaparrals, often shortened to "Chaps." They were named for the thorny bushes dotting the Texas landscape. The team's owners were among the wealthiest men in Texas. Unfortunately, they didn't spend a lot of money on their team. Most of their draft picks chose to play for the NBA instead. Higher-priced

GERVIN achieved his signature finger roll by flicking the ball off his fingertips and arcing it toward the basket.

veterans played elsewhere. The Chaps qualified for the playoffs in their first five seasons. But they never made a serious run at the championship. In 1972–73, they lost two-thirds of their games. Attendance was terrible. Just 134 diehard fans attended their final game that season. The owners were losing money.

A group of San Antonio investors agreed to "lease" the team for three years. This group wanted to change the team name to Gunslingers. But the group decided on Spurs instead. It was a less violent way of reflecting Texas's cowboy heritage. San Antonio fans loved their new team. The Spurs' first home game was on October 10, 1973. A raucous crowd of about 6,000 fans packed HemisFair Arena. It was a welcome surprise for the players. "It's great to play for these people," said guard Joe Hamilton. "They're rooting for us all the time."

Several ABA franchises besides Dallas were struggling financially. The Virginia Squires had serious issues. They sold their high-priced players during the 1973–74 season. The Spurs bought center Swen Nater from the Squires early in the season. He became Rookie of the Year. Then the Squires sold Gervin to the Spurs. He transformed the way the Spurs played.

The Spurs finished their first season at 45–39. They lost to the Indiana Pacers in the first round of the playoffs. The fans still loved them, though. In fact, the Spurs drew larger crowds than their fellow Texans, the Houston Rockets. The Rockets played in the NBA. The San Antonio investors tore up the lease. They bought the team outright from the owners in Dallas. Now the Spurs were completely San Antonio's team. They rewarded their fans by winning 51 games in 1974–75. They won 50 the following year. But they still couldn't pass the first round of the playoffs.

DUTCH TREAT

SWEN NATER, CENTER, 6-FOOT-11, 1973–75

Swen Nater was born in the Netherlands. His parents moved to America when Swen was six years old. They couldn't afford to bring him. Three years later, the television show *This Is Your Life* reunited the family. "I went from an orphanage to a Beverly Hills [California] hotel in 22 hours," he said. Eventually, he received a scholarship to UCLA. His role was pushing All-American center Bill Walton in practice. "No one outworked me, not even Bill. I had fun challenging Bill. I gave him everything he could handle," Nater said. The Milwaukee Bucks made him their top pick in the 1973 NBA Draft. Nater chose the ABA. He joined the NBA when the ABA folded. He is the only player to be the rebounding leader in a season in both leagues.

SPURRED INTO THE NBA

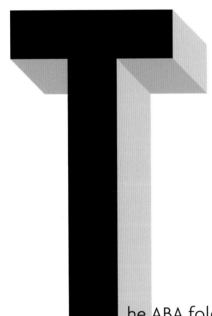

he ABA folded in 1976. The NBA invited San Antonio and three other teams with good attendance records to join them. The Spurs played in the league's Eastern Conference. They didn't miss a beat

A slender powerhouse, **GERVIN** led the league in scoring for four years.

The Spurs could not dodge the Bullets in a tight, seven-game playoff series in 1979.

18

in their new league. San Antonio averaged 115 points a game in the first season. That was the best in the NBA. The Spurs had a 44–38 record. But the Boston Celtics eliminated them in the first round of the playoffs. In 1979, San Antonio finally won a playoff series. It knocked off the Philadelphia 76ers in seven games. It took a 3–1 edge over the defending NBA champion Baltimore Bullets in the conference finals. But the Bullets fired back. They won the next two games by four and eight points respectively. Game 7 was especially discouraging. The Bullets pulled out a two-point victory with eight seconds remaining. Gervin performed well the next season. He won his third-straight scoring championship. He averaged more than 33 points a game. But San Antonio sagged to 41–41. It exited the playoffs in the first round again.

The Spurs moved to the Western Conference the following season. They won the Midwest Division three years in a row. Twice they advanced to the conference finals. Both times they lost to the Los Angeles Lakers. A combination of coaching changes and injuries hampered the Spurs in the 1983–84 season. The 37–45 mark was the team's first losing season in San Antonio. It was also the first time the Spurs missed the playoffs. They improved to 41–41 the following season. They lost in the first round of the playoffs. Team management decided to rebuild. They traded Gervin.

MAKING HISTORY

ALVIN ROBERTSON, SHOOTING GUARD, 6-FOOT-3, 1984–89

A quadruple-double is a rare feat. It means a player has double-digit tallies in four of five categories. These are points, rebounds, assists, steals, and blocked shots. Alvin Robertson is one of just four players to ever notch a quadruple-double in a game. On February 18, 1986, the Spurs beat the Phoenix Suns, 120–114. Robertson recorded 20 points, 11 rebounds, 10 assists, and 10 steals. He is the only one to have steals as the fourth category. "I feel happy and excited about the stats, but winning the game is most important," Robertson said. "A win is the ultimate satisfaction I can get."

21

One of the key building blocks of the rebuilding team was young guard Alvin Robertson. He had been San Antonio's top choice in the 1984 NBA Draft. "The Spurs were always known as a high-scoring offensive team led by Ice [Gervin]," said coach Cotton Fitzsimmons. "But we needed toughness and quickness. Alvin gave us that look." Robertson had an average rookie season. But he warmed up in his second year. He became the first winner of the league's Most Improved Player award. He played in the All-Star Game. He was voted Defensive Player of the Year. He also averaged 17 points a game. It wasn't enough. The Spurs still posted losing records.

THE ADMIRAL COMES ON BOARD

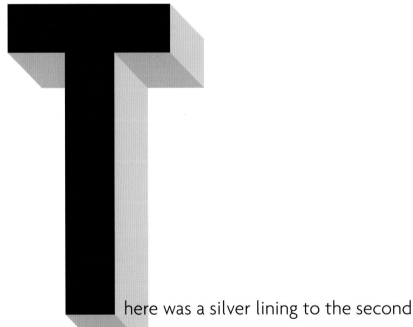

There was a silver lining to the second losing season. San Antonio received the top overall

Towering center **DAVID ROBINSON** took command of the struggling Spurs in 1989.

ROBINSON spent his entire career with the Spurs, earning All-Star status 10 times.

"[ROBINSON] HAS THE TALENT ALL US BIG GUYS ONLY HOPE AND DREAM FOR. NO OTHER BIG GUY I'VE EVER SEEN IS ANYWHERE NEAR AS QUICK AND FAST AS HE IS."

pick in the 1987 NBA Draft. The Spurs selected David Robinson. He was a 7-foot-1 center from the U.S. Naval Academy. He had been College Player of the Year. Robinson had to fulfill a two-year service obligation with the navy. Team officials felt he was worth the wait. In the meantime, the Spurs continued losing. They won just 21 games in 1988–89. It was the worst mark in team history.

Then Robinson arrived. He was nicknamed "The Admiral." The Spurs soared to 56 wins. It was a 35-game improvement over the previous season. That set an NBA record for the biggest single-season improvement. Robinson averaged 24 points, 12 rebounds, and 4 blocked shots a game. He was named Rookie of the Year. He also won the IBM Award. A computer formula determined the winner. "He has the talent all us big guys only hope and dream for," said Spurs backup center

Caldwell Jones. "No other big guy I've ever seen is anywhere near as quick and fast as he is." Rookie small forward Sean Elliott also played a major role. Like Robinson, he had been College Player of the Year. He was named to the All-Rookie second team. Unfortunately, the Spurs lost to the Portland Trail Blazers, four games to three, in the second round of the playoffs. Two losses came in overtime.

ith the Admiral commanding the San Antonio fleet, the Spurs became consistent winners. But they struggled in the playoffs. They lost in the first round in three of the next four years. They advanced to the second round in 1993. But the Phoenix Suns eclipsed them, four games to two. People said that San Antonio lacked "killer instinct." The team traded Elliott for Dennis "The Worm" Rodman. He and Robinson were the league's "Odd Couple." Robinson was very

Stealthy guard **SEAN ELLIOTT** seemed to cover the entire court all at once.

28

strait-laced. Rodman dyed his hair and plastered tattoos all over his body. Robinson was smooth. Rodman was scrappy. He fought for every rebound. He won the league's rebounding title in 1993–94. Robinson was the NBA's top scorer. It was the first time teammates had won these honors in the same season. Robinson scored 71 points in one game. He was just the 4th player to reach the 70-point level.

The Spurs went full speed ahead in the following season. They won a franchise-best 62 games. Robinson was named the NBA's Most Valuable Player (MVP). He received his third IBM Award. San Antonio cruised through the first two rounds of the playoffs. It faced the Houston Rockets in the Western Conference finals. The Spurs suffered a heartbreaking loss in Game 1. Rockets forward Robert Horry drained a shot with six seconds left. Houston won, 94–93. The Rockets also won Game 2. San Antonio battled back to even the series. But the Rockets took the next two games. The Spurs won 59 games in 1995–96. But the season ended on a sour note. They lost to the Jazz in the second round of the playoffs. Injuries sank the team the following season. San Antonio won only 20 games.

LEGENDS OF THE HARDWOOD

POUNDING THE BOARDS

DENNIS RODMAN, SMALL FORWARD, 6-FOOT-7, 1986-93

Dennis Rodman may have been the NBA's greatest rebounder. He stood 6-foot-7. He weighed just 215 pounds. But he led the league in total rebounds four times. He likened himself to a computer. His "hardware" was his body. He had exceptionally long arms. Because he was wiry and agile, opponents had a hard time boxing him out. His "software" was how he studied his opponents. For example, he noticed that Shaquille O'Neal's missed baseline shots often bounced back to him. So, Rodman would run right at Shaq when he shot.

Always in control, **TIM DUNCAN** had a countermove for every one his opponents made.

CHAMPIONSHIP ERA

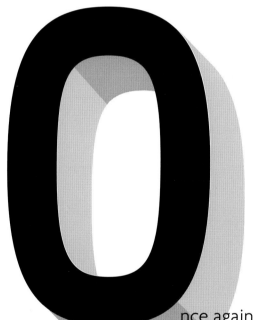

Once again, a terrible season resulted in a terrific draft choice. The Spurs took power forward Tim Duncan with the top choice in the 1997 NBA Draft. "Once he gets more comfortable, he's going

POP GOES SAN ANTONIO

GREGG POPOVICH, COACH, 1996–PRESENT

Gregg Popovich considered a career with the Central Intelligence Agency (CIA). Instead, he turned to coaching. He became the Spurs' head coach in 1996. The team won just 20 games. Two years later, San Antonio won its first NBA title. Since then, it has added four more. "I think you have to have accountability," he said. "For us, the thing that works best is total, brutal, between-the-eyes honesty. I never try to trick a player or manipulate them, tell them something that I'm going to have to change next week." Many people list "Pop" as one of the greatest coaches in NBA history. He is just one of three men named Coach of the Year three times.

LEGENDS OF THE HARDWOOD

to be unbelievable," said Robinson. "He can score on the block, he's got great post moves, and he's a great passer." Like the Admiral, Duncan quickly picked up a nickname. He had superb fundamental skills. People called him the "Big Fundamental." Also like Robinson, he sparked a huge turnaround. The Spurs improved to 56 wins. Duncan was an easy choice as Rookie of the Year. There was another reason for the team's success. It was Gregg "Pop" Popovich's first full year as head coach. Still, the Spurs couldn't get past the second round of the playoffs.

The Spurs had the NBA's best record the following season. They dominated the playoffs. They lost only one game in the first three rounds. They demolished the New York Knicks, four games to one, to win their first-ever NBA championship. "Defense won it for us," said Robinson. "This championship sends a message that persistence and

34

Point guard **TONY PARKER** was the first foreign-born player to make the NBA's All-Rookie team.

hard work can pay off." They were just as persistent and hardworking in the next three seasons. But a return to the championship series eluded them. San Antonio added more pieces to an already talented lineup. Point guard Tony Parker was the team's top draft choice in 2001. Argentine star shooting guard Manu Ginobili came aboard the following season. The Spurs advanced to the NBA Finals after the 2002–03 season. They defeated the New Jersey Nets, four games to two. Robinson retired. He was among a handful of NBA players to score more than 20,000 points and haul down more than 10,000 rebounds.

Speedy guard **MANU GINOBILI** was named the NBA's Sixth Man of the Year for 2007–08.

FROM THE POOL TO THE HARDWOOD

TIM DUNCAN, POWER FORWARD/CENTER, 6-FOOT-11, 1997–2016

Tim Duncan grew up in the U.S. Virgin Islands. He dreamed of becoming an Olympic swimmer. But in 1989, Hurricane Hugo damaged the pool where his team trained. The coach moved the practices to the ocean. Duncan was terrified of sharks. He quit. His brother-in-law talked him into playing basketball. "[Duncan] was so huge," said the athletic director of the school he attended. "So big and tall, but he was awfully awkward at the time." By his senior year of high school, he had become a star. Wake Forest University offered him a scholarship. He graduated as the College Player of the Year.

LEGENDS OF THE HARDWOOD

> "YOU FOLLOW YOUR LEADER. TIMMY
> IS THE LEADER OF THE TEAM, AND
> HE JUST CARRIED US TONIGHT."

The Lakers knocked the Spurs out of the playoffs the following season. But San Antonio returned to the NBA Finals in 2005. The series against the Detroit Pistons went to the full seven games. The Spurs won a tight defensive battle in Game 7. "You follow your leader," said Parker of Duncan. "Timmy is the leader of the team, and he just carried us tonight." The Spurs set a franchise record with 63 wins in 2005–06. But they lost to the Mavericks in the second round of the playoffs. The decisive Game 7 went into overtime. The Spurs returned to the Finals the following season. There was no doubt this time. They swept the Cleveland Cavaliers in four games. The Spurs won Game 3 by three points and Game 4 by just one. It was their fourth title in nine years. "It never gets old, it never gets old," Duncan said. "Unbelievable. Such a great run, a great journey, a great bunch of guys."

38

KAWHI LEONARD displayed dynamic defending and efficient shooting early on.

STAYING ON TOP

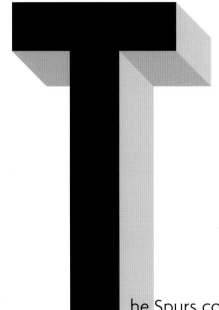

he Spurs continued playing at a high level. They won at least 50 games every season. One reason was the addition of young players such as Kawhi Leonard. He was named to the All-Rookie first team

The Spurs topped the league with 62 wins in 2013–14 and doused the Heat to take the title.

in 2011–12. In 2012–13, San Antonio easily advanced to the NBA Finals. It lost to the Miami Heat in a seven-game series. The following season was a rematch. This time, the Spurs won the championship, four games to one. In the 2014–15 season, the Los Angeles Clippers knocked them out of the playoffs in the first round.

Before the 2015–16 season, the Spurs signed free agent power forward/center LaMarcus Aldridge. He was a four-time All-Star with Portland. He helped the Spurs notch a spectacular 67–15 record. Only six teams have won more games in a season. In any other year, that mark would have attracted considerable attention. But all eyes were on Golden State. The Warriors set an all-time NBA record of 73 wins. Fans eagerly anticipated a historic matchup in the Western Conference finals between the two teams. It didn't happen. The Spurs routed the Oklahoma City Thunder in the first game of the conference

LaMARCUS ALDRIDGE added scoring and rebounding punch to San Antonio's offense.

44

KEEP ON TRUCKING

KAWHI LEONARD, SMALL FORWARD, 6-FOOT-7, 2011–PRESENT

No one doubted Kawhi Leonard's defensive ability when he joined the league in 2011. His offense was another matter. He averaged only eight points a game. People were surprised when Spurs coach Gregg Popovich said, "I think he's going to be a star. And as time goes on, he'll be the face of the Spurs, I think." Popovich was right. By the 2015–16 season, Leonard averaged more than 20 points a game. He ranked second in three-point shooting percentage. His defense was even better. With a huge multi-year contract, Leonard had no financial worries. Yet he still drove a 1997 Chevy Tahoe truck. "It runs," Leonard said, "and it's paid off."

semifinals, 124–92. The Thunder rallied to win four of the next five games. Two wins came in San Antonio. During the entire season, the Spurs had lost just once at home. "It was a surprising result not only because the Spurs dominated Game 1, but because they had so clearly established themselves as the NBA's second-best team all season," said sportswriter Eric Freeman.

The Spurs retained that position in 2016–17, with 61 wins. Leonard had an MVP-caliber season. But both he and Parker were injured as San Antonio faced Golden State in the conference finals. The dominant Warriors swept the series.

The last time the Spurs didn't qualify for the playoffs was 1996–97. As of 2017, their streak was at 20. They could break the all-time record of 22. Some people have tried to make the case that the Spurs are the most successful NBA franchise. After 2016–17, they had winning records in 36 of their 44 seasons. They have five championship titles. Only three franchises have more: Boston (17), Los Angeles (16), and Chicago (6). Spurs fans look forward to moving up this ladder.

SELECTED BIBLIOGRAPHY

Ballard, Chris. *The Art of a Beautiful Game: The Thinking Fan's Tour of the NBA*. New York: Simon & Schuster, 2010.

Hareas, John. *Ultimate Basketball: More Than 100 Years of the Sport's Evolution*. New York: DK, 2004.

Hubbard, Jan, ed. *The Official NBA Basketball Encyclopedia*. 3rd edition. New York: Doubleday, 2000.

NBA.com. "San Antonio Spurs." http://www.nba.com/spurs/.

Simmons, Bill. *The Book of Basketball: The NBA According to the Sports Guy*. New York: Ballantine, 2009.

WEBSITES

DUCKSTERS BASKETBALL: NBA

http://www.ducksters.com/sports/national_basketball_association.php

Learn more about NBA history, rules, positions, strategy, drills, and other topics.

KAWHI LEONARD DEFENSE: LOCKDOWN HOW TO

https://www.youtube.com/watch?v=6UipM10DdG0

This video analyzes the factors that make Kawhi Leonard such a great defender.

Note: Every effort has been made to ensure that any websites listed above were active at the time of publication. However, because of the nature of the Internet, it is impossible to guarantee that these sites will remain active indefinitely or that their contents will not be altered.

INDEX